MW00965705

SURVIVAL SKILLS HANDBOOK

FOREST

Bear Grylls

This survival skills handbook has been specially put together to help young explorers like you to stay safe in the wild. Forests and woodlands can be found all over the world and, with plenty of food and water, and lots of fascinating plant and animal life, they are perfect places to go exploring. This book is packed with top tips to help you stay safe on any forest adventure – so get out there and explore!

Bear

CONTENTS

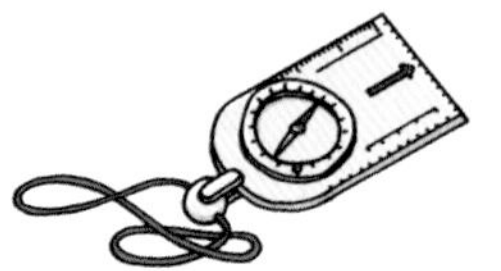

FORESTS OF THE WORLD

Forests are areas of dense trees. Some are quite small, while others cover a vast area. They contain many natural resources, but you will still need good survival skills to live in a forest for any length of time.

Forest types

Forests cover nearly one-third of Earth's dry land. There are several types of forest. The two main types are broadleaved and conifer forests. There are also mixed forests where both types of trees grow.

Broadleaved forests

Broadleaved forests grow mainly in temperate (mild) parts of the world, where seasons change throughout the year. Broadleaved (deciduous) trees, such as oak and beech, shed their leaves in autumn and are bare in winter. In spring, they grow new leaves. This means conditions vary a lot in broadleaved forests.

Conifer forests

Conifer forests grow mainly in cooler parts of the world. Conifer trees have narrow, waxy leaves that stay on the tree all year round. In winter, these forests provide shelter for wildlife, but the soil is poor, so few plants grow below the trees.

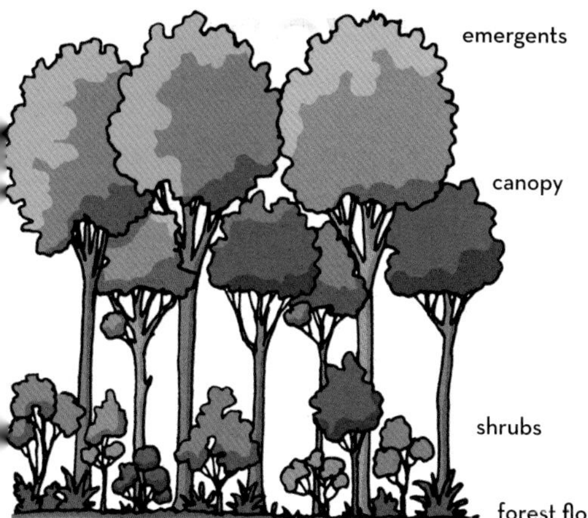

Storeys

Scientists studying forest life divide forests into vertical layers called storeys. At the very bottom is the forest floor, with a shrub layer of low-growing plants above this. Trees grow up and create a leafy layer called the canopy. Finally, a few taller trees poke up above the canopy. These trees are called emergents.

Resources and survival

Most forests have abundant food, water, and timber for fuel and shelters. However, the dense trees make navigation difficult. You will need your wits about you to make your way through a forest!

BEAR SAYS

Forests can only grow in places with high levels of rainfall. Expect showers and take full rain gear on a trip to the forest. Conditions are often muddy, so wear boots.

RAINFORESTS

Rainforests grow in places that get a lot of rain – over 200 cm a year. There are two main types of rainforest: tropical and temperate rainforests. You will also find montane or "cloud forests" in uplands, and mangrove forests on coasts. Food and water are abundant in these forests, but there are dangers too.

Tropical rainforests

Tropical rainforests grow close to the Equator. Here, conditions are hot, wet, and steamy all year round. Rain falls on most days. The world's largest rainforest, the Amazon, covers about half of South America. Vast rainforests also grow in west and central Africa and southeast Asia.

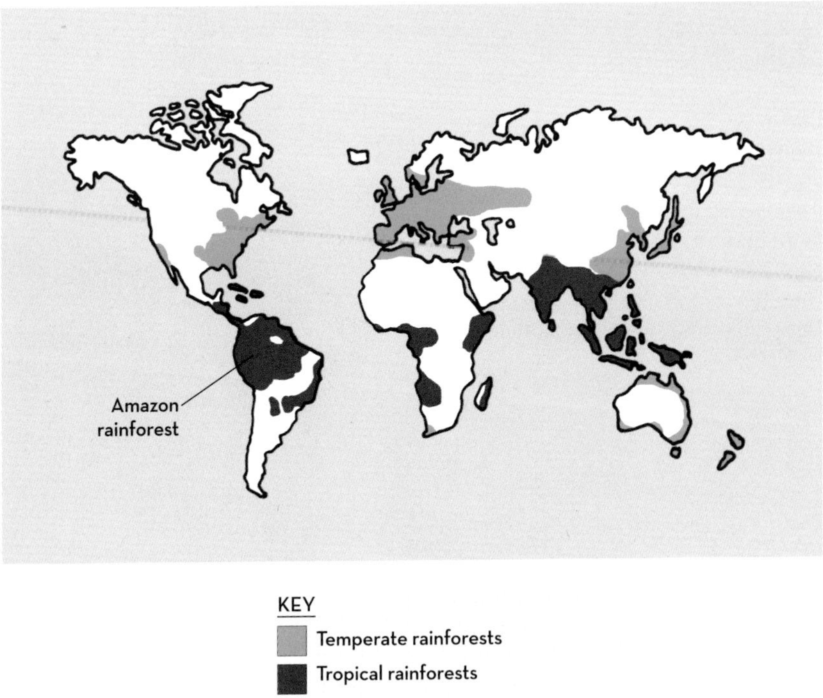

Amazon rainforest

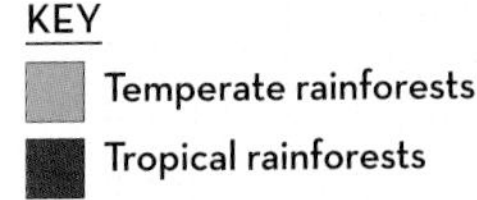

Temperate rainforests

Temperate rainforests grow in cooler parts of the world, north or south of the tropics. These forests grow along the west coast of North America, and also in Chile and New Zealand. They once covered a larger area, but huge swathes have been cut down.

Giant trees

North America's temperate rainforests contain some of the world's tallest trees: giant redwoods and sequoia. These mighty trees grow up to 106 m tall. Australia's dry forests contain eucalyptus trees, which also grow to enormous heights.

Deforestation

Timber is a very valuable resource. The world's tropical rainforests are disappearing fast as trees are felled for timber, or to make way for farms and ranches. Forest land is also cleared to dig mines and build roads, towns, and villages. This affects local wildlife and even the climate. This problem is called deforestation.

BEAR SAYS

Tropical rainforests contain many dangerous creatures, from jaguars to poisonous snakes and minibeasts. If you are camping, tip out your boots in the morning, in case a centipede or scorpion has crawled in during the night!

THE TAIGA

A vast belt of coniferous forest stretches across North America, Europe, and Asia, south of the Arctic tundra. Up to 800 km wide, it's known as the taiga – the Russian word for forest. Taiga conditions are particularly harsh in winter, which makes it hard to survive here for very long.

Climate and conditions

The taiga has long, cold winters, with temperatures dropping to –50°C. Snow covers the ground for months at a time. The most common trees here, such as spruce and fir, are cone-shaped, which allows snow to slide off them. In summer, temperatures rise above 10°C. Much of the snow melts, making the ground marshy.

BEAR SAYS

In summer, snowmelt forms pools and marshes in northern forests. Take a staff or walking pole if walking here, and use it to check the water depth in front of you. Move slowly and cautiously, and never go alone.

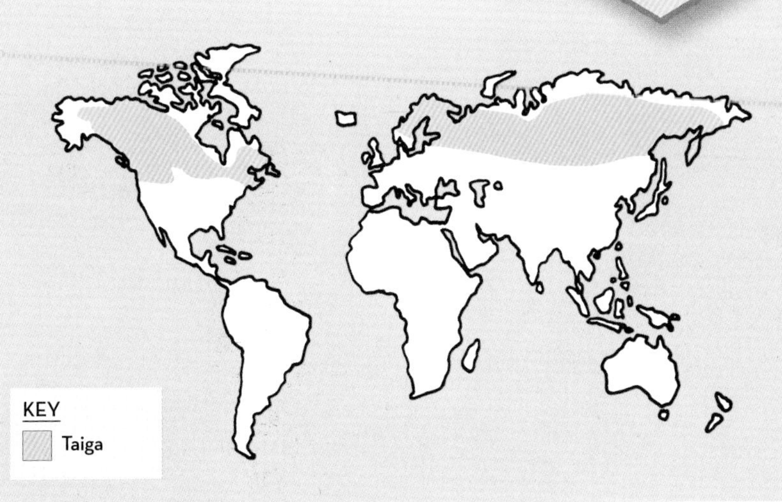

Wildlife

Reindeer spend the summer months feeding on the Arctic tundra. In autumn, they move south to spend winter in the taiga, where conditions are more sheltered. These forests are also home to stoats, foxes, squirrels, and fierce wolverines.

Way of life

The harsh climate means that few people live in the taiga. Some earn a living by hunting, fishing, logging, or reindeer herding. People traditionally lived a nomadic life, moving their herds from place to place and camping in tents made of animal hide.

Escaping from a marsh or swamp

1. Keep calm. Don't struggle or try to lift your feet clear, as you will only sink in deeper. Get rid of any kit that is weighing you down.
2. Look around for the nearest firm ground, or an overhanging branch that you can use to haul yourself to safety.
3. Spread a rucksack, shirt, or jacket in front of you, then slowly tip yourself onto it.
4. Try to get one leg to the surface, then monkey-crawl your way out.

1

3

2

4

CLOTHING AND EQUIPMENT

Good preparation is vital for a forest expedition. The right clothing and equipment will keep you dry and comfortable. With a tent, supplies, and a fire-making kit, you can survive for days.

Clothing

Packing several thin layers of clothing is better than one thick layer. That way, you can take off or add an extra layer as needed. The outer layer should be fully waterproof.

Check the weather forecast to fine-tune your equipment before setting out. Pack spare clothes in a plastic bag so they stay dry for when you need them!

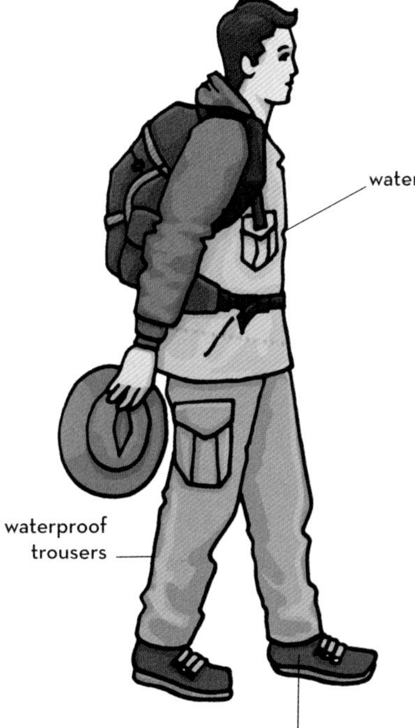

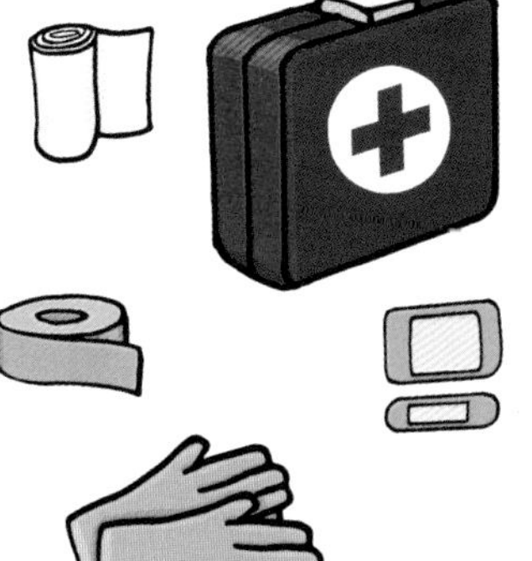

First aid

A portable first aid kit should include bandages, plasters, medical tape, scissors, disposable gloves, safety pins, and painkillers.

quipment

Rucksack

Don't pack so much gear that your rucksack becomes heavy and uncomfortable. Pack items such as your map, compass, and mobile phone in pockets that will be easy to reach.

Camping kit

FOREST MAMMALS

Many forests contain large mammals that can be dangerous. Luckily, these wild animals are mostly shy, and keep well away from humans. They are very unlikely to attack unless you disturb them, or if they decide you are a threat.

Moose and elk

Moose and elk are the largest members of the deer family. They are wary and mostly avoid people, but stags (males) can be more aggressive in the breeding season, so find out when this is before setting off.

Wolves

Wolves hunt in packs in northern forests. Attacks on humans are very rare, but if they threaten you, don't turn your back and run – wolves can easily outrun you! Wave your arms and shout to appear as big and fierce as possible. Avoid eye contact. Climb a tree or onto a high rock if possible.

Bears

Bears are omnivores. This means they eat both meat and plants. Large, brown bears called grizzlies may see you as prey. Mothers with cubs are particularly dangerous, as they can be very aggressive when protecting their babies.

Skunks

These medium-sized mammals are armed with a foul-smelling liquid, which they squirt from glands near the anus. If a skunk does a handstand, beware – it's preparing to squirt you! Back away – fast!

Porcupines

These large rodents are armed with sharp spines called quills. They clatter their teeth and rattle their quills to warn intruders away. They can charge, but cannot shoot their quills.

BEAR SAYS

Make a lot of noise as you move through the forest to scare bears away. Camp food attracts bears like a magnet, so store it high above the ground (see pages 16–17).

What to do in a bear attack

If you see a bear, back away slowly. Don't turn your back, and don't look at the bear directly. Wave your arms above your head and shout. If attacked, play dead, or blast it with pepper spray. If all else fails, jab it in the eye or punch its snout.

FOREST MINIBEASTS

Forests are home to myriad smaller creatures such as frogs, reptiles, insects, and spiders. Some of these are armed with venom; others can deliver painful bites or stings. Watch where you step, and take care when touching rotten wood.

Snakes

Less than half of all snakes are venomous, but some are extremely dangerous. Learn to identify the species that live in local forests. If you are bitten, bind the area above the bite and hold it lower than your heart to reduce the spread of venom. Seek medical help immediately.

Amphibians

Some frogs have poisonous skin to ward off attackers. Brightly coloured species are likely to be poisonous, so don't eat them.

Mosquitoes

In some parts of the world, these insects transmit deadly diseases such as malaria. Use tropical-strength insect repellent and keep your skin covered. Try not to scratch insect bites, as that will make them itchier. You may need to take malaria medication before you travel to certain areas.

Ants and wasps

Woodland insects that live in colonies can be aggressive. A wasp sting can be fatal if you have an allergic reaction. Avoid disturbing nests, whether in a tree or underground.

Ticks

These tiny relatives of spiders bury their head in their victim's flesh and suck their blood. They can also carry disease. Remove a tick carefully with tweezers, taking care not to detach the head as it will get stuck in your skin.

Leeches

Leeches live in water and damp places. They attach themselves to your skin and suck blood. Pick a leech off by hand before it gets anchored, or use salt or a flame. Sterilize the wound to avoid getting an infection.

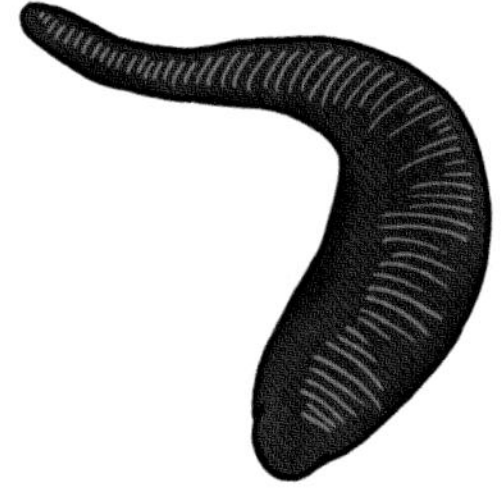

Spiders

Some spiders deliver a painful bite, and a few forest species are lethal. Some large, hairy tarantulas can shoot stinging hairs. Research the species that live in your forest.

BEAR SAYS

If you run out of insect repellent, a smoky fire can ward off mosquitoes. Smear mud on exposed skin, and cover your head, for example with a shirt.

FOREST CAMP

Forests are sheltered places, but you will still need protection from wind, wet, and cold if you plan to camp overnight. Choose your campsite carefully, and spend time setting up and organising camp.

Good campsites

Scan the forest for the best campsite. A forest clearing will be warm and sunny. Don't camp under a dead tree or dead branch that could fall and injure you. A fallen tree might make a good windbreak. Try to find level ground, as it will make your night much more comfortable.

Sites to avoid

Choose a site close to water, but not in a valley bottom that could flood after rain. Avoid still water where mosquitoes breed. Caves offer good shelter, but be cautious as you enter, as animals may lurk inside.

Preparing the ground

Choose a flattish site. Clear away debris such as sticks, stones, and pinecones, which will be very uncomfortable to lie on!

Erecting tents

Hammer in pegs using a stone or mallet. Go gently – try not to bend the pegs. Guy-ropes can be tied to saplings unless it's very windy, when a powerful gust could rip the fabric.

Camp layout and hygiene

Plan your camp layout. The cooking site should be close to water. Site the toilet away from and downstream of the cooking area. Wash your hands thoroughly after going to the toilet and before touching food.

Divide tasks if camping in a group. Everyone should do their fair share of chores. Decide on a place to keep tools and equipment, and make sure everyone returns them after use.

Caching food

In forests with bears, you will need to store food high in a tree. Seal food in airtight containers, bag it, and attach a rope. Loop the rope over a high branch. Suspend the bag about 3 m off the ground and well away from the trunk.

Building a debris hut

Forests contain lots of materials for shelter-building. With a bit of time and effort, you can build a shelter that will keep you reasonably warm and dry.

You will need:

pine or spruce branches, moss, grass, or ferns

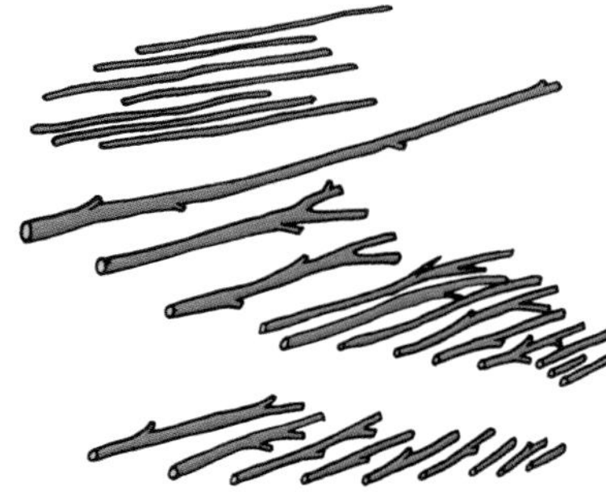

sturdy branches of various sizes

Making a bough bed

1. Lie on the ground and mark your body length. Use four straight sticks to mark the edges of the bed. Hammer in pegs or sharpened sticks to secure the poles.
2. Pile pine or spruce branches in the bed to form a thick mattress. Pile dry moss, grass, or ferns on top.

BEAR SAYS

A debris hut can catch fire quite easily – it's a giant heap of dry tinder! Site a fire well away from your hut. Don't build the hut bigger than you need – it just wastes time and resources.

1

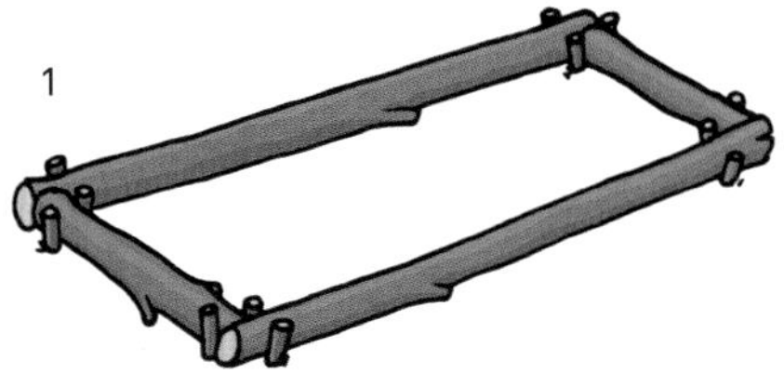

2

Debris hut step-by-step

You will need: several sticks, including a long, straight stick for the ridgepole.

1. Select two stout, forked sticks about 1 m long. Wedge them together to form an A-shape. Bind with string or rope if you have any, and drive the ends into the ground.
2. Remove any side branches from the ridgepole and place one end on the A-frame, with the other anchored firmly in the ground.
3. Lay several shorter sticks vertically against the ridgepole on both sides, leaving a gap for the entrance.
4. Weave branches through these uprights to form a mesh. If desired, you can wedge and weave smaller sticks to form a covered porch above the entrance. Cover the structure with a layer of moss and leaves to a depth of about 50 cm.
5. Pile dry, soft material such as leaves, ferns, and moss inside, or make a bough bed.

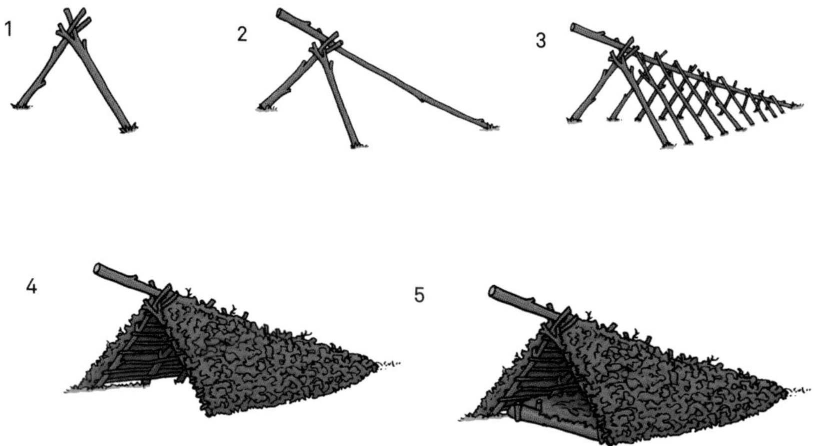

Making a forest bivouac

You will need two tarpaulins and some rope to rig this jungle-style bivouac. Construct the frame securely so you can rig the bed above the ground, out of reach of creepy-crawlies.

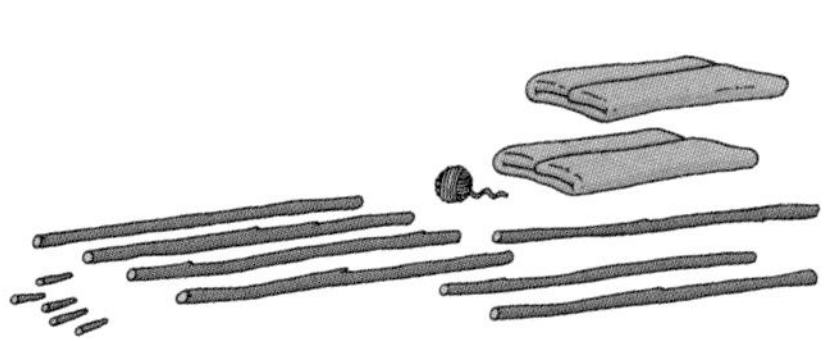

1. Collect all materials before you start. You will need seven long, stout, straightish poles, all strong enough to take your weight, and two tarpaulins.

2. Remove side branches from the poles. Lash two poles together with rope to form an A-frame. Lash it to a tree for support.

3. Make a second A-frame, and position it about 2 m from the first. Use a guy-rope to secure it. Balance the ridgepole onto the two A-shapes and lash securely.

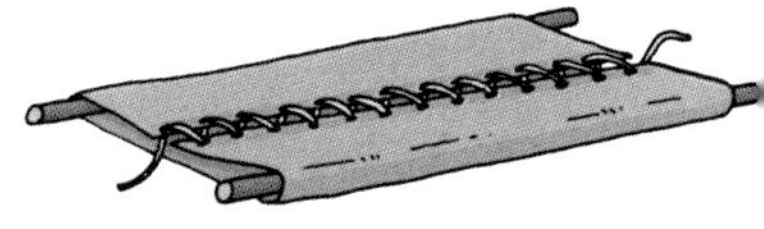

4. Fold one tarpaulin in half. Loop string between the eyeholes to form a tube. Insert the remaining two poles into the tube and pull it taut like a stretcher.

5. Wedge the poles of the stretcher on the outside of the A-frames. Spread the legs a little wider if the bed slips down. You can also wedge it above the stumps of cut-off branches on the frames.

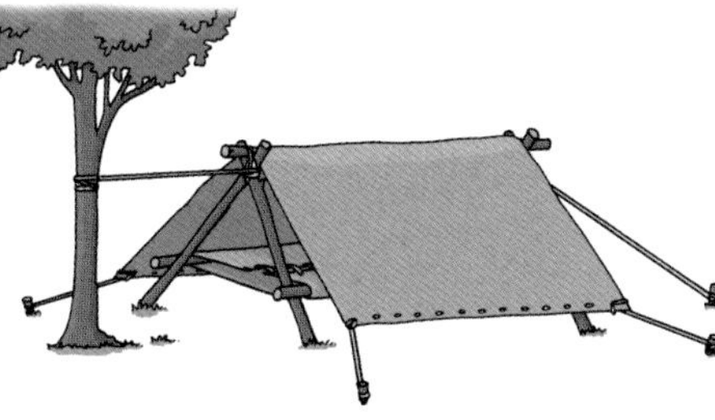

6. Throw the second tarp over the ridgepole. Attach rope or string to each corner and either peg it down or tie it to saplings.

Pine tree bivouac

In deep snow, the hollow space beneath a pine tree can provide a snug bivouac, out of icy winds. Dig under the lowest branches to reach the hollow, trying not to dislodge snow. Excavate the hollow as needed. Line it with a tarp or plastic, or use a bivvy bag.

FINDING WATER

Water is vital to your health – you can survive for only a few days without it. Water is generally plentiful in forests, but usually must be purified before it's safe to drink.

Collecting rainwater

Rainwater is often the safest drinking water, assuming you collect it in a clean container and don't let it stagnate. Tie a tarp between branches or to stakes driven into the ground, and place a stone in the centre. To harvest water, lift one end of the tarp to channel it into a container placed below.

Transpiration bag

Plants give off water through their leaves – this is called transpiration. Tape a clear plastic bag over a leafy branch in a sunny position. Tie the top with string. Moisture from the leaves will condense on the inside of the bag.

Tapping into a vine

Wild grape vines hold large quantities of fluid. Scrape the bark from a looping vine at its lowest point, then make a tiny cut on top. The dripping water is safe to drink.

Streams and pools

Collect water from fast-flowing streams. Place your container under a waterfall if there is one. Water from still pools and lakes is less pure, as it has had time to stagnate. Collect it from the surface, or where a stream enters the pool.

Purifying water before drinking

Filtered water must still be sterilized before drinking. Boil water in a pan for five minutes, or use a pump or sterilizing tablets.

Making a water filter

Cut off the top of a plastic bottle and tie a scrap of cloth over the neck. Turn upside-down and fill with layers of fine sand and gravel, then coarse sand and gravel. Hang from a tree and pour water through to filter it. You can also use a sock!

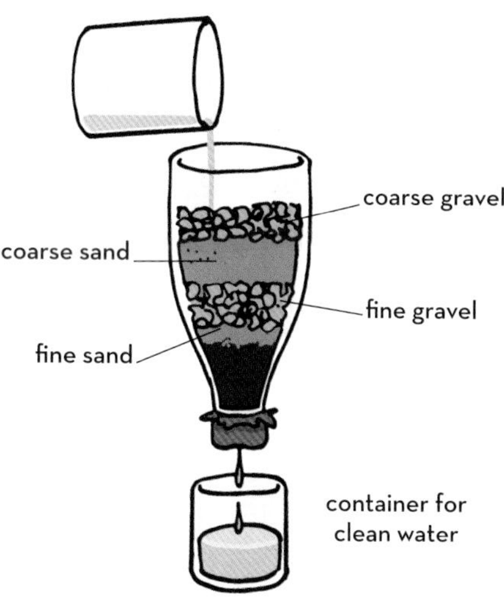

EDIBLE PLANTS

Forests contain many foods, such as berries, nuts, roots, and edible fungi. However, some plants and many fungi are poisonous, so be sure to positively identify species before you taste them.

Edible plants

Young, tender leaves of dock, dandelion, chickweed, and plantain can be boiled and eaten. The growing tips of red and black spruce and Arctic willow are edible too.

Nuts, fruits, and berries

Hazelnuts, pine nuts, and sweet chestnuts are delicious roasted. Horse chestnuts (conkers) are poisonous. Blackberries, cloudberries, wild cherries, and salmonberries can be eaten raw. Crab apples are better cooked. Avoid white or yellow berries: many species are poisonous.

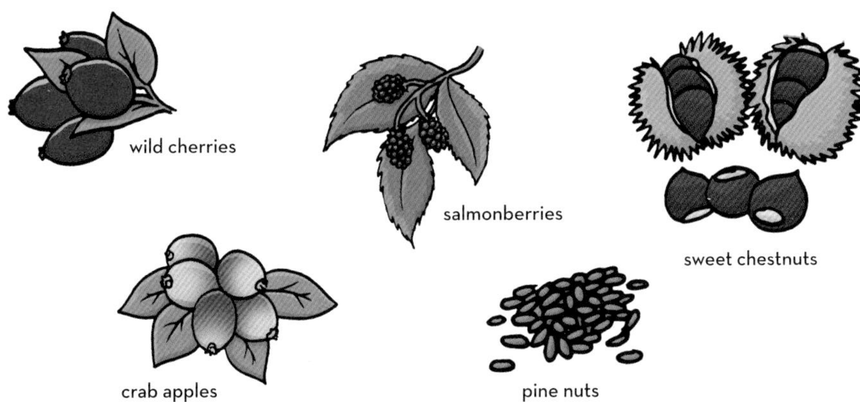

Poisonous plants

Deadly nightshade and hemlock are highly poisonous – learn to identify them. Also steer well clear of poison ivy, poison sumac, and poison oak – all produce a nasty skin rash.

hemlock

beefsteak fungus

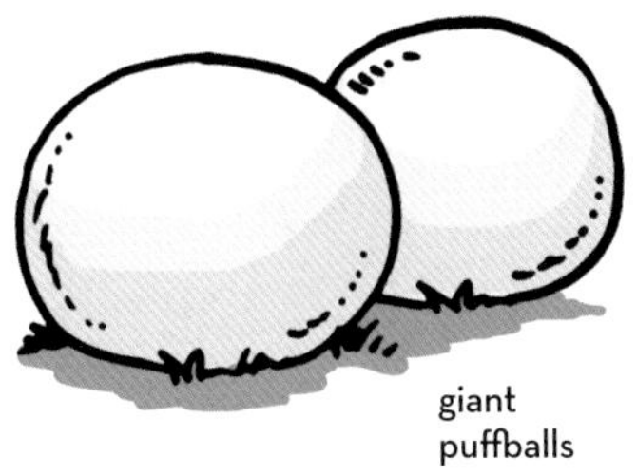
giant puffballs

Edible fungi

Beefsteak, oyster, and honey fungus grow on trees. All are edible when cooked, as are field mushrooms and giant puffballs.

Poisonous fungi

Many poisonous fungi grow in forests. They include fly agaric, death cap, and destroying angel. These last two are easily confused with edible mushrooms. If in doubt, don't pick them.

BEAR SAYS

Don't take any risks when foraging. Only eat wild foods if you are absolutely sure you can identify them. A guidebook to local plants will help with identification.

fly agaric

death cap

FISH AND GAME

In an emergency survival situation, forests have abundant fish and game that you can eat. Though you should only do this if you really need to, knowing how to track, catch, and cook different forest animals is a useful survival skill.

Animal tracks

Tracks in soft mud or snow show where animals pass regularly. Learn to identify tracks. You may also find tufts of hair on fences, claw-marks on trees, and remains of food, such as nibbled nuts.

deer

rabbit

Stalking animals

Move quietly and slowly when stalking. Wear dull-coloured clothing, and use cover such as bushes. Stay downwind of animals so they don't catch your scent. Avoid stepping on dry twigs or leaves that will snap or rustle to give you away.

squirrel

Slugs and bugs

The idea of eating insects, grubs, slugs, snails, and worms may not be appealing, but all are nutritious in a survival situation. Look for minibeasts under bark, stones, and logs, but beware poisonous species. Avoid brightly coloured beasties and hairy caterpillars. Wash and roast or boil before eating.

Making a fishing rod

Rig a fishing rod using a straight stick, string, and a hook made from a thorn or safety pin. Bait the hook with bread or with a live worm or maggot. Check the water depth and tie a float onto the line. The float will twitch when you get a bite.

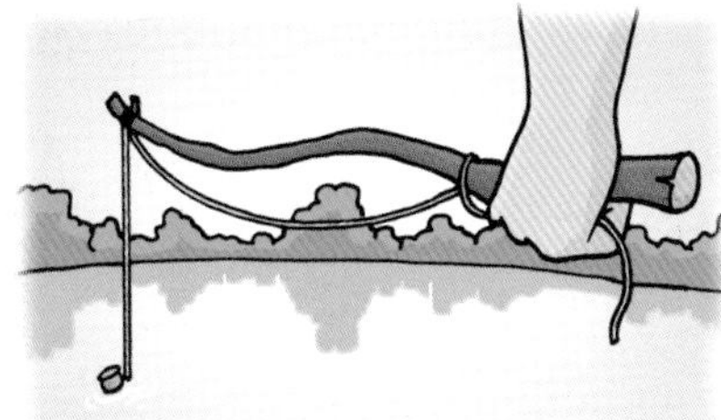

Cleaning a fish

Prepare a fish for cooking by carefully slitting the belly from tail to throat. Ease open and remove the guts without puncturing them. Remove the head, gills, and tail and wash before cooking.

BEAR SAYS

Tracking and catching game or fish is time-consuming and can be frustrating. You will probably try many times before you succeed, but the extra protein is worth the effort.

FOREST TOOLS

Sharp tools are incredibly useful in a forest. Knives, machetes, axes, and saws can be used for crafts and shelter-building, but all sharp tools must be handled with care. Clean and store tools after use so they don't get blunt or rusty.

Cutting tools

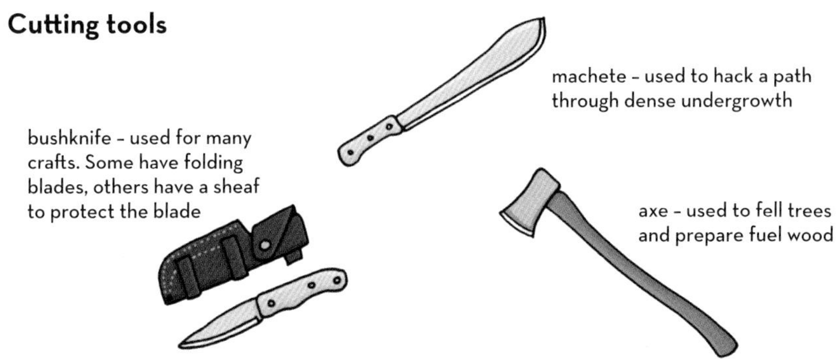

Using a machete

Make sure you have enough space to swing the machete safety. The wrist strap prevents it flying out of your grasp. Slash downwards at an angle. Using a machete is tiring, so take turns. Machetes are very dangerous, so it's best to leave them to a responsible adult.

Using a knife

Always cut away from your body. You can use a forehand or a backhand grip. Pass a knife handle-first and with the blade upwards. Never try to catch a falling blade.

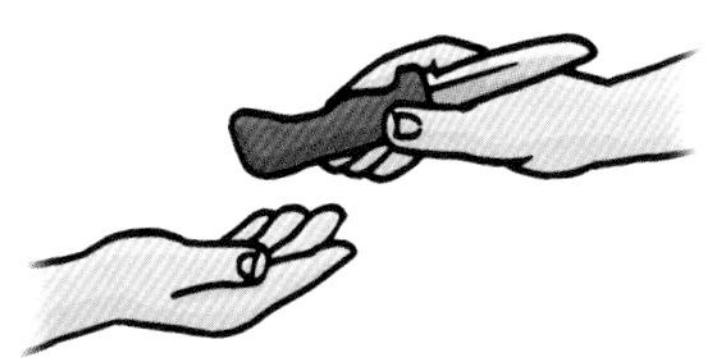

Chopping kindling with an axe

Stand the log on a block or tree stump. Aim to cleave it down the centre. If the wood doesn't split cleanly, raise the axe and the log, and strike down on the block.

Felling a sapling with an axe

Make two wedge-shape cuts in the trunk as shown in the picture on the left. The sapling will fall in the direction of the biggest wedge.

Using a saw

Place a log or branch on a stump or cut log, and hold it steady with your foot or spare hand as you saw.

Sharpening tools

The easiest way to sharpen a knife is with a leather strop. Hold the blade almost flat and draw the edge along the strop. Repeat about 10 times, keeping the angle the same. Turn the blade over and repeat. Sharpen a blunt blade on a sharpening stone (shown left) using the same technique.

CORDAGE

Cordage is string, rope, or cord. Forest peoples traditionally make cordage from natural materials. Practise this ancient skill and put it to good use around camp.

Making cordage

1. Gather a quantity of long, stringy plant stems, such as rushes, grasses, or vines such as honeysuckle. You can also use nettles (wear gloves and crush the stems to destroy the stinging hairs).
2. Roll two stems between your palms to twist the fibres. Knot one end. Lengthen the cord by splicing on another strand. Twist the fibres in the opposite direction to join the two, or plait them together. Plait three strands to make a stronger cord.

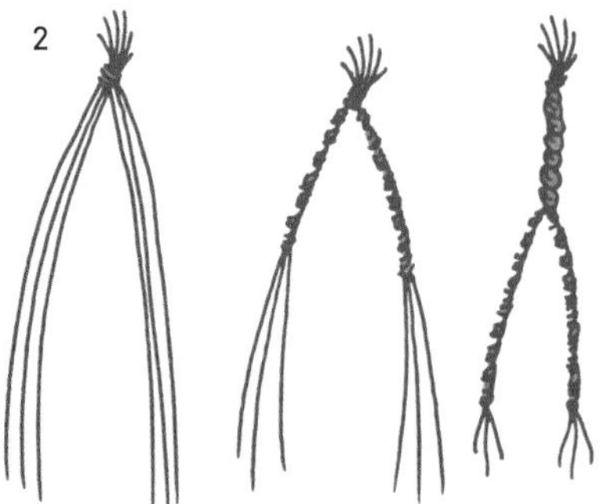

Overhand knot

Make a knot as shown and pass the end back through it.

Overhand loop

Loop over the end of the cord and tie an overhand knot over the loop.

Clove hitch

This knot secures a cord to a pole or branch.

1. Loop the cord over the pole, then bring the end in front and across itself.

2. Loop the cord around the pole again, then pull the end up and under itself. Pull the ends to tighten.

Square lashing

This knot secures two sticks or poles at right angles.

. Hold the sticks at right angles. Tie one end of the cord in a clove hitch to the bottom strut.

2. Wind the cord over and under the sticks as shown. Keep it taut.

3. Secure with a clove hitch at the top.

MAKING BIRCH BARK CONTAINERS

Birch bark is an amazing material. Tough and flexible, it's also waterproof. Many people who live in forests traditionally use birch bark to make containers. You can use other bark if no birch bark is to hand.

Identifying birch

Birch trees are slender, with pointed leaves, papery bark, and catkins in spring.

Making a birch bark box

1. Cut a rectangle of bark, as shown on the opposite page. Measure, mark, and cut a line of holes down the two short sides. The holes should be 2 cm apart and match exactly. Make the holes with a nail or by twisting with your knife.
2. Curl the bark into a circle. Line up the holes and thread string through to stitch it together. Pull tight and knot the ends.
3. Draw around the bark circle on a piece of flat wood 2–4 cm thick. Cut around the base with a knife, leaving a 1 cm border. Carefully trim the base so it fits snugly inside the bark circle. Glue the edges and gently tap into place.
4. If desired, make a wooden lid for the box by repeating step 3. Make a hole in the centre of the lid, thread cord through it, and knot the ends.

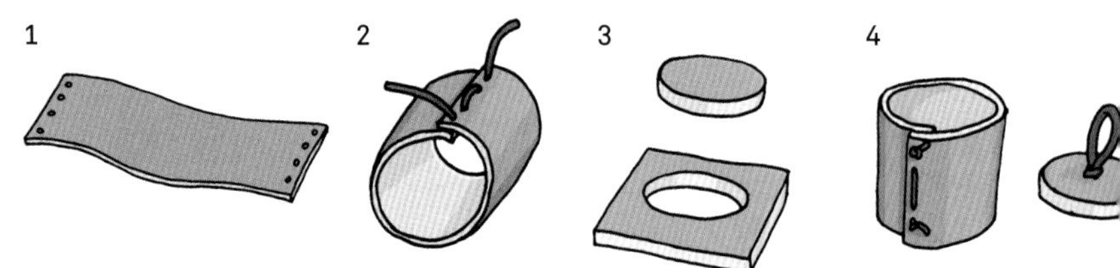

Making a bark bowl

This bowl can be used to collect water or gather food such as berries.

1. Harvest a rectangular piece of bark from a tree by cutting around and down the trunk. Don't cut right around the trunk, as this will kill the tree.
2. Insert the point of your knife and gently peel the bark away, taking care not to pierce it.
3. Make four pegs from green (freshly-cut) sticks. Cut pieces about 15 cm long. Using a penknife, carefully split the wood to half-way down, then wind string tightly above the split to seal it. Repeat to make three more pegs.
4. Make a diagonal fold in each corner of the bark rectangle. Fold over as shown and secure each corner with a peg.

BEAR SAYS

You can use bark from a fallen tree. Soak it in water overnight to make it pliable and easier to work with.

FIRECRAFT AND COOKING

A campfire provides light, warmth, and a means of cooking. It will dry wet clothes and ward off animals. However, damp conditions in forests can make it hard to get a fire going.

Gathering materials

You need dry tinder such as straw, kindling, and then small and larger wood to use as fuel. Gather these materials, dry them in the sun if needed, and store in a dry place.

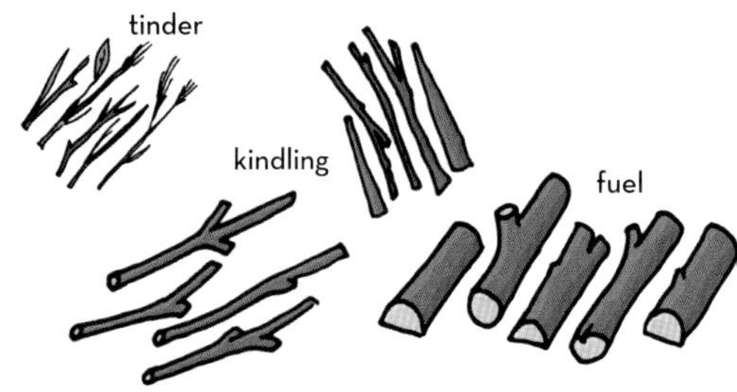

Preparing the site

Site a campfire downwind of tents so stray sparks don't ignite the fabric. A fallen tree makes a great windbreak. Find a flattish place and clear the ground of debris.

Making a fire platform

Fires are hard to light on damp ground. Build a platform with two layers of green sticks laid crosswise.

Tepee fire

A tepee fire is easy to build and light. Build a pyramid of kindling over a small pile of tinder, then set light to the tinder. Have larger sticks ready to feed the fire.

Scout fire

Build a tepee fire between two large logs to contain and shield the fire.

Fire-lighting

The easiest way to ignite a fire is using matches or a lighter. Cup your hand to shield the flame. You can also use a fire steel. Place the rod over the tinder and draw the striker along the rod to produce a spark.

Rigging a tripod

Bind one end of three long, straight sticks. Splay out the legs to make a tripod. This structure can be used to hang a kettle or pot over the fire.

Campfire cooking

There are many ways you can cook food over a campfire, including wrapping it in foil and placing in hot embers, or holding your food above the flames on a toasting fork or sharpened stick.

FIRE SAFETY

Fire can be very destructive in forests. In dry, windy conditions, stray sparks can start a blaze which then spreads quickly. Follow these safety tips when lighting a campfire in a forest.

Fire prevention

Have a bucket of water or sand standing by in case you need to put out the fire. On a campsite, note the location of extinguishers. Never leave a fire unattended. Be extra careful if you keep a fire going overnight.

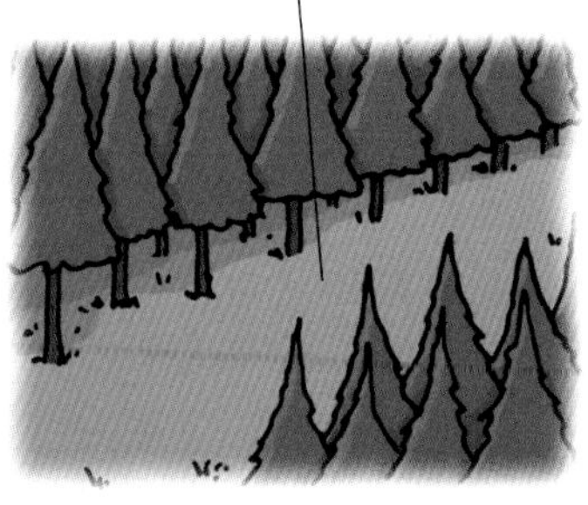

Forest fires

If you spot a forest fire, note the wind direction by watching the smoke. If the fire is upwind, you will need to move fast to escape it. Head away from the fire, preferably downhill to the safety of a lake or river, or head for a broad path called a firebreak – these are designed to prevent fire spreading. If overtaken by the fire, try to reach a burned-out patch, or seek safety in a ditch.

Putting out a small fire

Some forests have racks of fire brooms or spade-like rubber beaters. Note the location of these. Stamp out a small fire, or bring the broom or beater down to starve it of oxygen. Don't try to tackle a larger fire – it's far too dangerous.

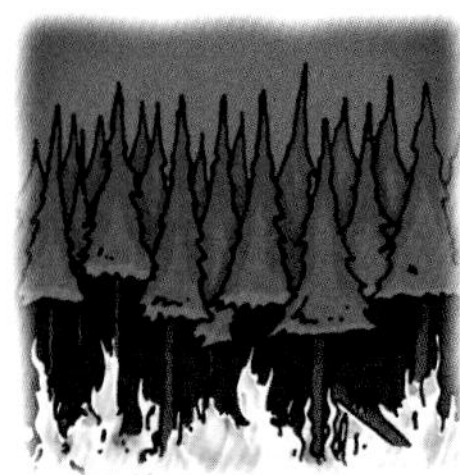

Escaping through fire

If you have to cross a fire to reach safety, tip water over your clothes and put a jacket over your head. Choose the best place to cross, take a deep breath, and cover your nose and mouth with a wet cloth.

1. Stop

2. Drop

3. Roll

Putting out burning clothes

If your clothes are on fire, roll on the ground or wrap yourself in a coat to smother the flames. If another person's clothes are on fire, throw them to the ground and follow the same steps.

BEAR SAYS

When breaking camp, make sure your fire is completely out by pouring water over it or smothering it with earth. Don't use leaf litter, which will reignite the flame.

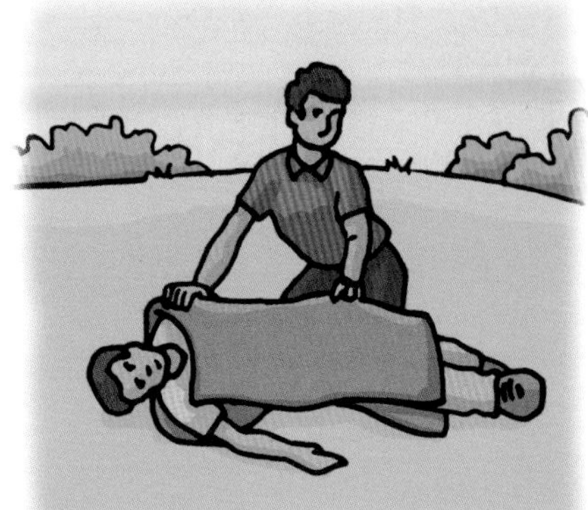

WOODLAND NAVIGATION

Getting lost is a serious hazard in forests, where trees and bushes create similar views in all directions. Brush up on your map and compass skills before a forest expedition.

Map symbols

Maps use symbols to show tree types, paths, streams, buildings, and other features. The key (panel) on one side explains the symbols. Not all maps use the same symbols, so check the key before you start out.

campsite

coniferous forest

footpath

marsh

deciduous forest

scrub

telephone

viewpoint

Map scales

Maps are drawn to different scales, as shown in the key. A small-scale map shows a large area. A large-scale map shows a small area in more detail. You can use the scale to work out how long it will take to walk between two points

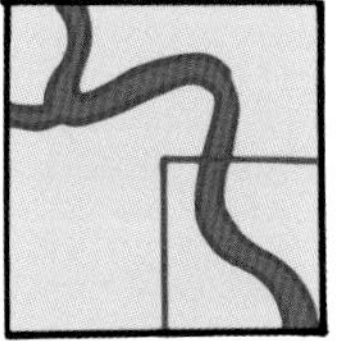

Grid references

Most maps have a grid of lines, which can be used to pinpoint locations. East-west distances are given first, then north-south distances. Read the grid reference by running your finger sideways along the map, and then up the side.

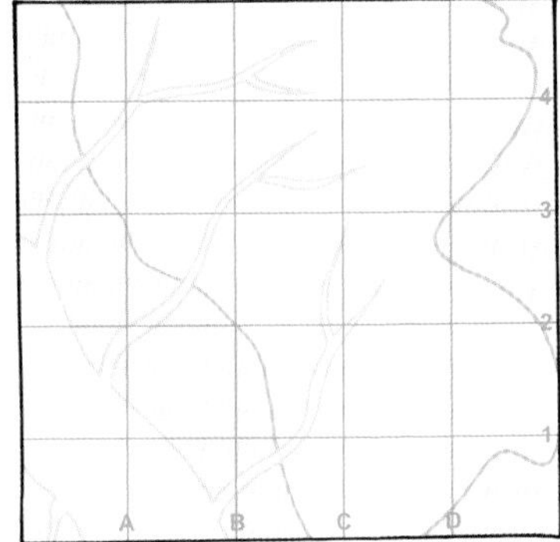

Compass

The red magnetic needle of a compass always points north. You can use that to work out other directions. Hold the compass level and keep it away from metal objects that may distort the reading.

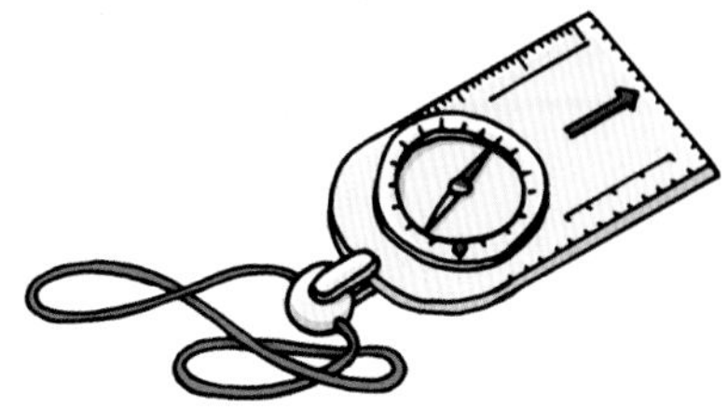

Using a compass with a map

1. Place the edge of the compass along your line of travel.
2. Turn the inner dial so the vertical lines match the north-south lines on your map.
3. Lift the compass off the map. Turn around until the red magnetic needle rests over the inner dial arrow. The direction of travel arrow now shows your bearing (direction).

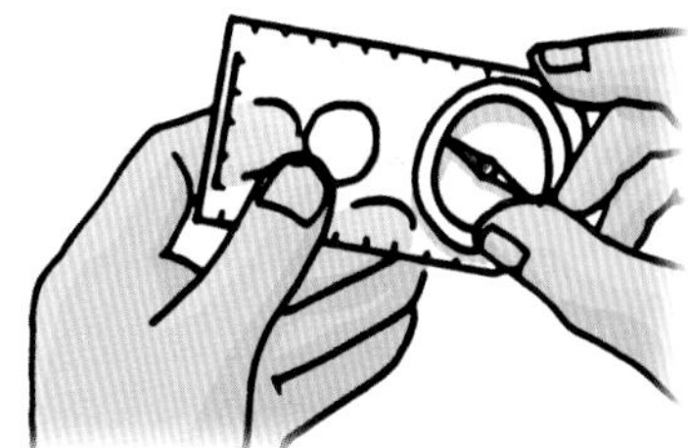

BEAR SAYS

Forests often have more paths than are shown on the map. Maps only mark official paths such as bridleways. In many countries, official paths are marked on the ground with signposts.

Navigation challenges

It's hard to make your way straight through a forest. Paths twist and turn, and fallen trees, streams, or swamps may block onward progress. The tips on this page will help you keep on course.

Spying out the land

Spy out the land whenever you get the chance. A hilltop, cliff, or clearing may allow you to see the way forward. If necessary, you could climb a tree.

Keeping on a bearing

In a group, send a scout forwards on the bearing. Check your compass and shout directions if they stray off the bearing. Stop them within earshot, catch up, and repeat.

Detour around an obstacle

1. Using your compass, turn 90° and walk parallel to the obstacle. Count your paces.
2. Once clear of the obstacle, turn back 90° and continue on your original course.
3. Turn a further 90° and walk the same number of paces as in step 1, to get back on your original bearing.

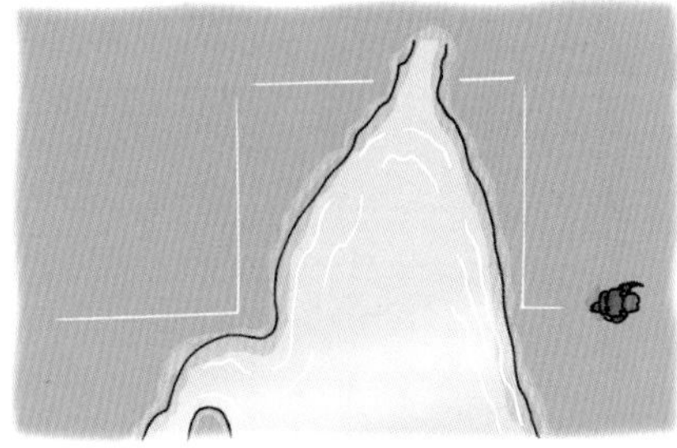

Keeping on track

It's easy to get lost in a forest because many places look the same. Notice landmarks you pass and note your progress on the map. You could use trail signs to mark your route (see pages 44–45).

Lost?

If you do get lost, keep calm. Consult your GPS or the map app on your phone if you have one. If separated from a group, you should probably stay put, so the others can come back for you. If alone, retrace your steps to the last place you recognize. Try to work out where you are on the map.

BEAR SAYS

Forest travel is often slow. You may only cover a few kilometres a day in dense jungle or trackless forest. Don't be overambitious when you plan a journey.

Finding north without a compass

In the northern hemisphere, snow lingers on the north side of trees, which is always in shadow. In North America, the leaves of the compass plant point north and south.

ON AND BY WATER

Forests contain many streams and rivers, thanks to the high rainfall. These features can be useful for navigation, but can also bar your way. The tips here will help you navigate and cross safely if needed.

Following a water course

Settlements are often built on streams and rivers. If you get lost, heading downstream may eventually lead to civilization. Streams and rivers marked on maps can also help you find your way.

Where to cross?

If a stream or river blocks your path, scout along the bank for the best place to cross. Don't try to cross on a bend, where the current will flow swiftly. Rocks may form stepping stones, but can be also slippery, with swirling water on all sides.

Tree bridge

A fallen tree can provide a bridge over water. You may also be able to position long, stout branches across a stream to form a makeshift bridge.

Group crossings

Don't cross alone if you can cross with others. In a group, you can either form a line or link arms to make a huddle, facing inwards.

Solo crossings

If you have to cross alone, use a stout stick to balance. Use the stick to check the depth of the water before you take a step. Go slowly and carefully test every step before you put your full weight on it.

Boots provide grip when crossing slippery rocks. However, if crossing firmer ground such as a gravel bed, you could remove boots to keep them dry.

Making a float

Crossing fast-flowing water with a rucksack is dangerous. The weight could throw you off balance and weigh you down if you fall. Wrap your rucksack in a plastic bag or tarp, and bind tightly with rope. The rucksack can now act as a float.

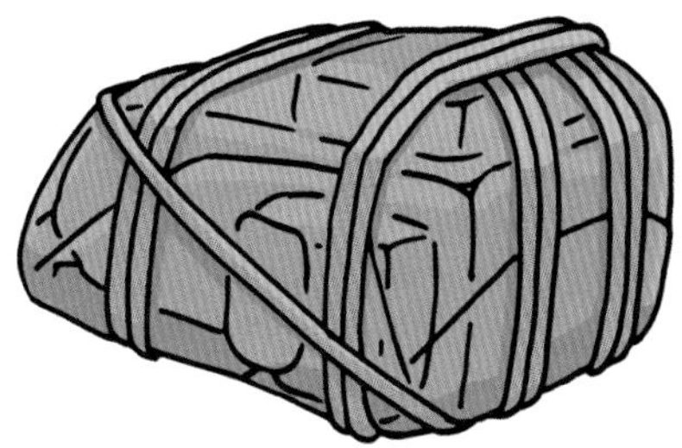

SIGNALLING IN FORESTS

Signs and signals can be used in forests to communicate with group members. You can also contact the rescue services in an emergency. Learn and practise signalling before a forest expedition.

Hand signals

Hand signals are useful at close range in a forest, particularly if you're tracking an animal and need to keep quiet. Here are some useful hand signals.

Numbers

one

two

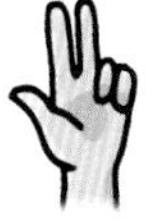

three

four

five

six

seven

eight

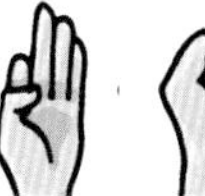

nine

ten

Movement hand signals

come here

hurry

stop

meet here

go here

wait

Actions hand signals

listen

look

cover this area

I understand

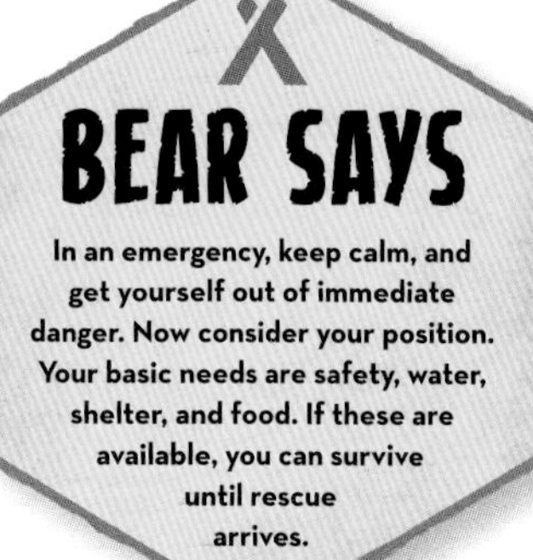

Trail signs

Scouts use trail signs to mark the route and communicate with others following behind.

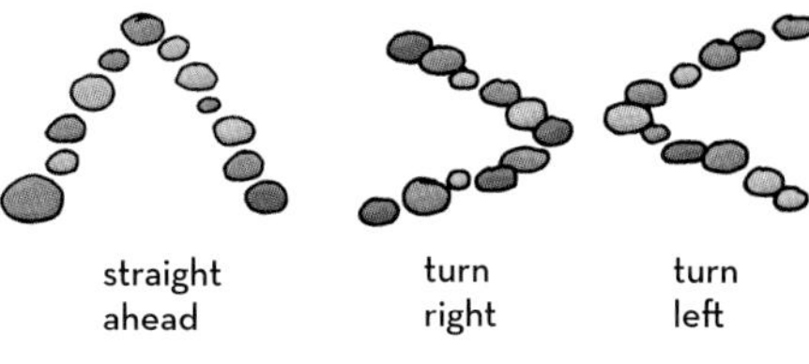

don't go this way

Calling for help

In an emergency, you may need to contact rescue services. Use your mobile phone if it has a signal. Be ready to give your name, details, and a grid reference or description of your location. Remember, SOS calls are taken very seriously, and should only be used in a real emergency.

Signalling with a whistle

Sound signals carry beyond the range of visual signals. All group members should carry a whistle. Work out a code to communicate, e.g. five long whistle blasts could mean return to base. Three whistle blasts is an international distress call.

Build a signal fire

Signal fires and smoke can be hard to spot from above a dense forest. Light a signal fire in a clearing or on a hilltop. Alternatively, construct a small raft and build a tepee fire on it. Anchor the raft in midstream and be ready to light the fire if a plane appears.

GLOSSARY

Bearing – The direction in which you are headed, as shown on a compass.

Bivouac – A temporary camp without proper shelter. Shortened to "bivvy".

Cache – A hidden food store, or to store food in a hidden place.

Canopy – The dense, leafy layer of interlocking branches in forests.

Conifer – A tree that produces seeds in cones. Most conifers are evergreen.

Cleave – To cut in half.

Deciduous – Broadleaved trees that shed their leaves in autumn and sprout fresh ones in spring.

Deforestation – Loss of forest when trees are cut down.

Distress signal – A call for help in an emergency.

Emergent – A tall tree which sticks up above the canopy in a forest.

Excavate – To dig out or remove loose material such as earth or snow.

Firebreak – A wide path in a forest designed to prevent fire spreading.

Foraging – Searching for wild foods.

GPS – Global Positioning System. A radio navigation system.

Grid reference – Numbers referring to the grid squares on a map.

Hemisphere – One half of the Earth, as divided by the Equator.

Ignite – To set light to something.

Kindling – Small fuel such as thin sticks, used to feed a newly lit fire.

Omnivore – An animal that eats both plants and animals.

Protein – A nutrient found in foods such as meat, fish, milk, eggs, and nuts.

Ridgepole – The long, horizontal pole of a tent which supports the fabric.

Storeys – The vertical layers of life in a forest, from the tallest trees down to the ground.

Taiga – The vast belt of forest that stretches across the northern hemisphere.

Tarpaulin – A thick, waterproof cloth, usually with eyeholes in the corners for attaching. Often called a "tarp".

Tinder – Very fine fuel used to catch a spark to light a fire.

Transpiration – Process by which a plant gives off moisture through its leaves.

Tropics – The hot regions on either side of the Equator.

Tundra – The cold, treeless plains of the far north.

Understorey – The layer below the canopy in a forest.

Visual – Relating to sight.

Discover more amazing books in the Bear Grylls series:

Perfect for young adventurers, the *Survival Skills* series accompanies an exciting range of colouring and activity books. Curious kids can also learn tips and tricks for almost any extreme situation in *Survival Camp*, explore Earth in *Extreme Planet*, and discover some of history's greatest explorers in the *Epic Adventures* series.

Conceived by Bonnier Books UK
in partnership with Bear Grylls Ventures

Produced by Bonnier Books UK
Suite 3.08 The Plaza, 535 Kings Road,
London SW10 0SZ, UK

BONNIER BOOKS UK
Editor Susie Rae
Designer Shahid Mahmood
Contributor Jen Green
Illustrator Ian Upstone

2 4 6 8 10 9 7 5 3 1

Disclaimer
Bonnier Books UK and Bear Grylls take pride in doing our best to get the facts right in putting together the information in this book, but occasionally something slips past our beady eyes. Therefore we make no warranties about the accuracy or completeness of the information in the book and to the maximum extent permitted, we disclaim all liability. Wherever possible, we will endeavour to correct any errors of fact at reprint.

Kids – if you want to try any of the activities in this book, please ask your parents first! Parents – all outdoor activities carry some degree of risk and we recommend that anyone participating in these activities be aware of the risks involved and seek professional instruction and guidance. None of the health/medical information in this book is intended as a substitute for professional medical advice; always seek the advice of a qualified practitioner.